THE TALENT MANAGE/ POCKETBOOK

G000256040

By Andy Cross
Drawings by Phil Hailstone

"An invaluable guide for line managers, full of practical advice and thought-provoking questions. All managers will be able to develop their own talent for attracting, retaining and developing their best people."
Dr Jane Yarnall, Director, Skills Evolution Ltd

"Jam-packed with excellent suggestions for how we, as managers, can integrate talent management into our daily working lives. It takes a common sense approach and smashes the myth that talent management is something done to or for us. Instead, it reinforces the view that we have as much responsibility to focus on this as, for example, on managing the bottom line. Well worth a read!"
Lin Kendrick, OD & Development Director, Virgin Media

Published by:
Management Pocketbooks Ltd
Laurel House, Station Approach, Alresford, Hants SO24 9JH, U.K.
Tel: +44 (0)1962 735573   Fax: +44 (0)1962 733637
E-mail: sales@pocketbook.co.uk
Website: www.pocketbook.co.uk

This edition published 2007.

© Andy Cross 2007.

British Library Cataloguing-in-Publication Data.
A catalogue record for this book is available from the British Library.

ISBN 978 1 903776 476

Design, typesetting and graphics by **efex ltd**. Printed in U.K.

CONTENTS

THANKS FROM THE AUTHOR

I have worked with talented people, in superb organisations, for many years as a leader, recruiter, coach, student and friend. In this book I have included just some of the ideas, beliefs and techniques I have learned and used to help talented people get great results. I love nothing better than watching enthusiastic people achieve more than they ever expected, especially my kids!

My thanks to:

Paul Tizzard	Louise Harrison	Moira Nangle
Richard Lowe	Sharon Brockway	Sir John Whitmore
Frank Dick	Helena Clayton	Adela Cross

In my work I have read widely and been influenced by many people. There is a list of great books at the back which I thoroughly recommend. My apologies if I haven't accurately referenced where other people have directly influenced what I have written.

FOREWORD

SOME WORDS FROM FRANK DICK, OBE

I've been fortunate to work with some of the most talented people in sport and business. Not everyone will be able to achieve world beating performances, but every one of us can take control of our performance and achieve a little bit higher than we did the day before.

Andy shares my passion for bringing out the potential in people, releasing them to be the best that they can be. I hope that you share this passion too.

This book is a great start point for anyone wanting to better understand how to manage talent. In reading this book you are taking the next step towards being the best you can be, and helping others do the same.

Keep smiling,

Coaching has been Frank's raison d'être for decades, inspiring world-beating performances from some of the top names in sport – Daley Thompson, Boris Becker, Gerhard Berger, Denise Lewis, Marat Safin and Katarina Witt. In business, he has helped develop a coaching culture in Barclays, BT, Unilever, Shell, Abbey and Rolls Royce.

INTRODUCTION

Imagine the following:

- ✔ Everyone on your team performs at the highest level every day
- ✔ You are constantly amazed by the no longer hidden talents of your team and their natural desire to perform at their best
- ✔ The best people look for opportunities to work on your team
- ✔ You make good choices so your new recruits blend in quickly with the team
- ✔ People thrive around you and are ready for the next challenge at just the right time
- ✔ When people do move on you can celebrate because they have prepared their own successors
- ✔ Your people leave as advocates for your organisation
- ✔ Some people return to continue their journey with you

Imagine you are a superb manager of talent.

Too good to be true? Probably. Something to aim for? Absolutely.

INTRODUCTION

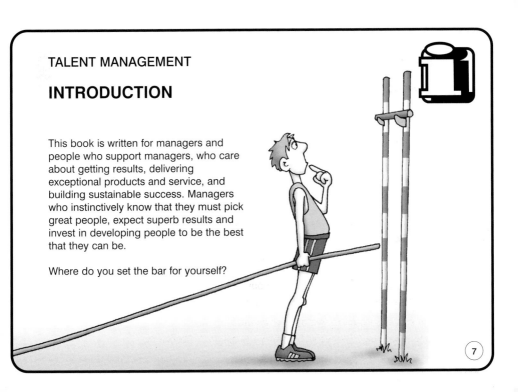

This book is written for managers and people who support managers, who care about getting results, delivering exceptional products and service, and building sustainable success. Managers who instinctively know that they must pick great people, expect superb results and invest in developing people to be the best that they can be.

Where do you set the bar for yourself?

TALENT MANAGEMENT

HOW TO USE THIS BOOK

This book introduces the Talent Web: five distinct roles that constitute great talent management (see diagram on page 24). Each role has a 'big' question!

Role	Big Question
Talent Spotter	What talent do I need and how can I spot it?
Talent Coach	How can I bring out the best in my people when it matters most?
Talent Blender	How can I blend the available talent to get maximum performance?
Talent Conductor	How can I create a flow of talented people?
Talent Magnet	What will attract talented people and keep them for longer?

The book has a section on each role which includes ideas, techniques and beliefs. You may read the book and feel comfortable with what you already do. If so, congratulations; I ask you to share your talent with others. I hope you will find nuggets to improve your own approach. Once you find these, the next step is to prioritise and plan the changes you want to make and enlist the help of others.

You can jump straight into any part of the web. If you do this and get stuck you may need to come back to the start and read the first section on *The Talent Difference*.

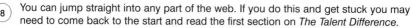

THE TALENT DIFFERENCE

FOCUS ON TALENT

Are you in a 'war for talent' or simply passionate about getting the best from your employees?

This section looks at the case for a greater focus on talent within your organisation.

THE TALENT DIFFERENCE

TALENT HEALTH CHECK

How important is managing talent to your organisation? Answer the following nine questions honestly to identify where a greater focus on talent management could improve your organisation.

	YES	NO
1. Have you found it difficult to fill a key role in the last 12 months?	◯	◯
2. Do you rely on external recruits for key roles?	◯	◯
3. Do you often compromise on quality at recruitment?	◯	◯
4. Have the challenges your team face changed in the last 3-5 years?	◯	◯
5. Are you worried that your organisation doesn't have the talent to grow?	◯	◯
6. Do your competitors appear to have stronger people than you?	◯	◯
7. When people are promoted, are they adequately prepared?	◯	◯
8. Do your best people often leave before promotion?	◯	◯
9. Are you often disappointed that your people don't achieve what you expected?	◯	◯

THE TALENT DIFFERENCE

TALENT HEALTH CHECK

Give yourself 1 point for each question you answered positively.

6 or more
✔✔✔✔✔✔
Your organisation is likely to either have significant cost or business risk associated with your approach to managing talent

4 to 6
✔✔✔✔
Your approach to managing talent is sometimes likely to create frustration and avoidable costs

3 or less
✔✔✔
The quality of your people probably gives you an advantage over other organisations; your focus will be needed to keep you ahead

How comfortable are you with the answers for your team or organisation? Which areas concern you the most? What strengths do you have on which to build?

Managing talent effectively must be a priority for any successful manager and business. So, what is the **talent difference**?

THE TALENT DIFFERENCE

WAR FOR TALENT

According to a report produced by two McKinsey consultants in 1998, there is a 'war for talent', a chronic shortage of talent across the board.

Trends	Impact
Increased competition and pace of innovation	Keeping ahead demands the best people
Influence of technology	Technology needs brainpower – a talent intensive asset
Flatter, leaner organisations	Slower promotions so external moves sought
More mergers, acquisitions and outsourcing	Loyalty to a single organisation continues to fade
Shrinking 25-45 year old demographics and many senior leaders approaching retirement	Smaller talent pool from which to select
Changing attitudes of people towards work	People are more demanding of an organisation to provide meaning, challenge and flexibility

Good organisations have always employed talented people but recent trends appear to have created a business imperative to focus on finding, developing, using and retaining talent – every manager, every business needs a 'talent mindset'.

THE TALENT DIFFERENCE

SHORTAGE OF TALENT

Is there really a shortage? Yes, according to most recent research.

An example:

- Average quality of candidates has declined by 10% since 2004
- Average time to fill a vacancy has increased from 37 to 51 days
- 30% of organisations have recruited below average candidates to fill a position quickly

Corporate Executive Board, 2005, International poll of 4000 hiring managers in 30 companies

Finding talent is undoubtedly getting harder, but what is the compelling case to manage talent better?

THE TALENT DIFFERENCE

SHIFTING THE BELL CURVE

Does a talent mindset really make a difference?

It is generally accepted that your best people will increase your operational productivity, profit and sales revenue significantly more than your average performers. Imagine the benefit to your business of shifting the overall performance 'bell curve' to the right.

Research* has shown that a shift in performance from the 50 percentile to the 86.5 percentile will lead to an average increase in financial productivity of 46% in highly complex and professional roles and at least 16% in basic clerical roles.

* *Hunter, Schmidt and Judiesch (1990)*

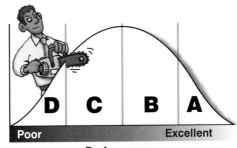

THE TALENT DIFFERENCE

SHIFTING THE BELL CURVE

Some organisations are rigorous in replacing the D's and retaining A's. Other organisations focus effort on defining the traits and attributes of the B's so that they can use this information to recruit more B's and develop the C's.

Some companies view every opportunity to replace someone as an opportunity to upgrade the quality of recruit.

In summary, any effective approach to attract, develop and better use talent has to be a good thing and any improvement in your ability to keep talented people for longer has to benefit the organisation.

TALENT IS CHANGING TOO!

There are several trends influencing the relationship between the employer and employee:

Bargaining power
Company loyalty cannot be assumed: shortage of talent provides greater bargaining power for the best people

Portfolio career
Companies are less able to provide long-term security so people see diverse expertise (portfolio careers) as an effective way to reduce risk

Greater meaning
People want greater meaning from their work

Flexibility
There is increasing desire to *work to live*, rather than *live to work*, and growing interest in more flexible working methods eg times and places

Fewer boundaries
Improved technology means that you don't have to be 'at work', or even in the country, to make a contribution

Informed choice
People are more aware of their market value and how different employers operate

THE RISK

A war for talent is a risky business; there is a potential 'dark side' to developing a talent elite.

Your best people will, undoubtedly, contribute greatly to your business. However, you may want to consider the following before you embark on any talent agenda:

> *"Fighting the War for Talent is hazardous to your organisation's health...a distraction from what companies should concentrate on... devising systems that get the most out of everyone."*
>
> **Professor Jeffrey Pfeffer**

- Do you value a deep knowledge of your organisation as much as a fresh perspective?
- Will focusing on high-flyers create an undervalued, cynical and demotivated core group?
- Do you define talent to include people outside your senior team – your *hidden* talent?
- Will your attempt to label talent denigrate others?
- Is your approach to talent providing equal opportunity or widening inequalities, eg: race, age, gender and sexual orientation?
- Have you looked at growing your own talent?
- Is your approach benefiting the wider community in which you operate?
- Are you stripping your industry of the most talented people without investing for the future?

EQUALITY OF OPPORTUNITY

Most people will accept the need to manage talent if it is coupled with an equality of opportunity, ie giving everyone a fair chance. Some indications that you take the dark side seriously include:

- You invest in people less fortunate outside your organisation
- You look at the future stream of talent (and customers) and provide incentives for people to educate/develop themselves further
- You create jobs and wealth in the groups who support your success

THE TALENT DIFFERENCE

WHOLE ORGANISATION

Your focus on talent must go beyond management capability and executive potential; **talent is not restricted to a level or status**. Increasingly, organisations are looking more widely to identify specific areas where there is a strategic business need. A whole organisation approach to talent starts with two questions: what differentiates you from your competitors now? What will keep you in that winning position?

Your answer could be any of the following:

- Great product design
- Exceptional customer service
- Brilliant planning and execution
- Superb sales and distribution
- Above average intellectual property
- Creativity and innovation

Identify your talent focus based on what differentiates your business. Once you know where to start, agree the unique abilities that will drive success and the specific issues you face. You can then segment your approach to talent and create your own map – now you know where to invest your efforts.

ANSWERING THE CYNIC

Some managers may want to bury their heads in the sand and ignore the debate. You may hit blockers, particularly when talking about developing your own talent in preference to recruiting externally.

Cynic: Why fuss about growing your own talent?

There is a world of talent out there and some of them already work for you! HR may deal with the impact of losing your best people and the cost of replacing them **but it is a business risk.** Don't get complacent; remember to treat your current staff with at least as much respect as people who have yet to prove themselves in your organisation.

Cynic: But our best people always want more money

Yes, and they will also want greater challenges, more recognition, exposure to your senior managers and for you to show a genuine interest in their future. If you are a skilled talent coach your investment will pay dividends.

THE TALENT DIFFERENCE

ANSWERING THE CYNIC

Cynic: And then they walk out the door

If you manage your talented people well they will stay longer and more than repay the time and effort you have invested in them. Your challenge is to act like a talent magnet, get everyone making a difference and keep the best for longer.

Cynic: Why worry; talented people will always rise to the top anyway

Possibly, but will it be in your organisation? As a talent coach you have a role to create a talent flow and make sure your people arrive at the next stage well prepared and quicker. If you leave it to chance, raw talent may stay raw!

Cynic: I've already got the best people so I'm OK

There is always someone more talented on your tail – you never have the winning formula for long. You need to be able to stay ahead, which means being creative enough to do today, what others will do tomorrow.

THE TALENT WEB

FIVE LINKED ROLES

Still reading? Do you recognise the talent difference and the contribution it will make to your business? Are you curious about your role in managing talent?

The rest of this book is based on the talent web – five linked roles that you need if you are to excel in this area.

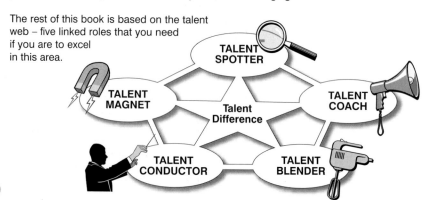

TALENT
SPOTTER

TALENT
MAGNET

Talent
Difference

TALENT
COACH

TALENT
CONDUCTOR

TALENT
BLENDER

THE TALENT WEB

FIVE LINKED ROLES

I've used the web analogy for several reasons:

- Each strand of the web is as strong as steel and incredibly sticky but has even more power when all the strands pull together
- Putting the first thread in place relies heavily on luck and the wind; after that each one can be quickly strengthened
- Incredible effort is needed to build the web but its reusability and ability to deliver make it a fantastic investment
- The web transmits vibrations through every strand to let you know it is working

THE BIG QUESTIONS

Each role in the talent web has its very own 'big' question.

Role	Big Question
Talent Spotter	What talent do I need and how can I spot it?
Talent Coach	How can I bring out the best in my people when it matters most?
Talent Blender	How can I blend the available talent to get maximum performance?
Talent Conductor	How can I create a flow of talented people?
Talent Magnet	What will attract talented people and keep them for longer?

Which of these questions can you answer now?

Which ones would you identify as priorities for you to answer?

TALENT SPOTTER

TALENT MAGNET

TALENT COACH

Talent Difference

What talent do I need and how can I spot it?

27

TALENT SPOTTER

DEFINITION

If you are going to make the most of your talented people you have to be able to recognise talent in the first place – you have to be a talent spotter. So, what does the word mean? Look for a definition using Google and you will get the following:

Main entry :	Talent
Part of speech :	Noun
Definition :	Ability
Synonyms :	Aptitude, aptness, art, capability, cleverness, command, flair, genius, gift, inventiveness, knack, know-how, mastery, power, savvy, skill, strength

1. A person who possesses unusual innate ability in some field or activity
2. Natural endowment or ability of a superior quality
3. A variable unit of weight and money used in ancient Greece, Rome and the Middle East. A talent of gold was double the weight of a talent of silver

BEING THE BEST YOU CAN BE

What do you look for when you are talent spotting? Ability, yes, but ability alone won't lead to enduring success. As they grow, even talented people need to have the courage to succeed or fail, to learn how to respond to defeat and how to bounce back. Sometimes talented people find life too easy and don't learn the lessons they need to succeed.

What qualities would be top of your list?

1st Passion to achieve
2nd Determination and perseverance
3rd Curiosity to learn and change
4th Ability

These translate into tough questions you should ask your team and yourself:

1. Do you want to succeed?
2. Do you believe you can succeed?
3. Will you keep going until you get there?

There are always people with more ability. The challenge for each individual is to have the passion, determination and curiosity to be the best **they** can be!

MINDSET

One of the most important factors when spotting talent is mindset, those people who go that little bit extra when it really matters. Frank Dick describes people as either Mountain or Valley people. Pay attention to what people say, what they do and how they respond to a challenge and you will soon know if you have a Mountain person on your hands!

Valley People

- Seek calm and comfortable ground and shelter
- Value safety and security
- Aim 'not to lose' so playing for a draw is OK
- Are fit to survive but little else
- Make excuses for not acting and believe others have all the luck

TALENT SPOTTER

MINDSET

Mountain People

- Take the risk of winning because there is no such thing as the risk of losing
- Aim to be the best they can
- Take personal accountability for their own performance
- Want to test ambition on the toughest climbs
- Will fight and endure discomfort to overcome difficulties

Adapted from *Winning: Motivation for Business, Sport and Life*, Frank Dick OBE

"You have to lean away from the mountain if you're going to learn to ski."

Anon

APPRECIATE YOUR TALENT

Everyone has talent but some hide it better than others. A healthy organisation will provide the opportunity for **every employee** to be the best that they can be.
Do you appreciate all of the talent in your organisation?

Within the scope of your team's ambitions, objectives and expectations, how do you define talent? Try this activity to start to define talent in your organisation:

Get together a cross-section of your employees, including senior managers, and ask the following appreciative questions:

1. Our best people can be described as....
2. The magic in our people usually shines when....
3. We are most successful in our organisation when...
4. Our future success depends on people who.....

Use the list you create or review your existing definitions of talent and agree what you must keep doing to find the talent you need.

IDENTIFYING TALENT

Where do you set the bar when defining talent? Is it the people who stand out from the crowd? The people with a genius for making things happen? The following definition builds on ability and includes the dimension of **impact** on you and others.

Talent is:

- A genius for making things happen…
- With a minimum fuss…
- Inspiring others to do the same

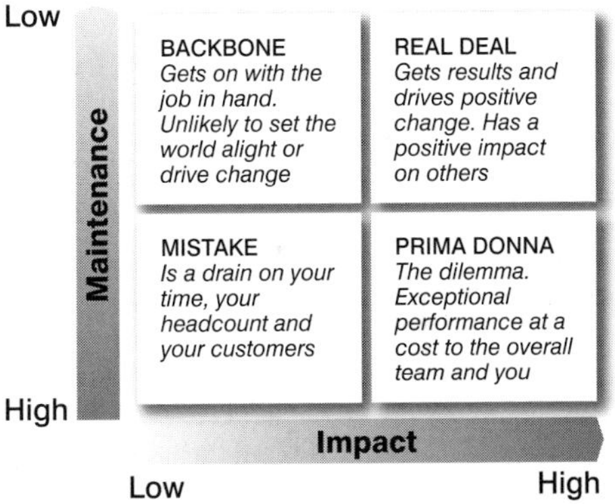

	Impact	
	Low	**High**
Low	**BACKBONE** *Gets on with the job in hand. Unlikely to set the world alight or drive change*	**REAL DEAL** *Gets results and drives positive change. Has a positive impact on others*
High	**MISTAKE** *Is a drain on your time, your headcount and your customers*	**PRIMA DONNA** *The dilemma. Exceptional performance at a cost to the overall team and you*

Maintenance (vertical axis, Low at top, High at bottom)

Talent is often associated with *prima donna* behaviour – explosive and attention-seeking but undeniably able to make a significant difference. The performances must be good enough to justify inclusion. Don't fall into the trap of assuming that the most visible and vocal people are the most talented.

(33)

TALENT SPOTTER

FLYING START

What does it take to get raw talent off to a flying start? Investing your time early pays dividends but do be careful not to stifle talented people. A fresh perspective doesn't last forever and being too directive and controlling can make it disappear even quicker. The best you can do for your new people is to give them opportunities to meet people and understand the business, ask them questions and provide constructive feedback.

1. Hold up the mirror – raise self-awareness by providing high quality feedback.
    A simple approach like **AID** usually works wonders:

A ction   What you have observed

I mpact   The implications of the action

D esired Outcome   What needs to be done next time

Remember the **AID** model can be used to frame positive feedback, with the 'Desired Outcome' being: **do it again!**

FLYING START

2. Help people **GROW** – ask questions that encourage improved performance:

G oals   What are you trying to achieve?

R eality   What's happening now?

O ptions   What could you do?

W hat   What are you actually going to do?

3. Get them clued up – organise a route map for the individual to find out how the organisation operates, the complexities of the industry and the customer and/or product experience.

TALENT CHAMPIONS

Every organisation has talent champions – the people who excel at finding hidden talent and helping them thrive. Who are yours?

Cheerleaders   Excellent at pushing people into the limelight and getting recognition for those with potential

Bridge Builders   Have the magical ability to open doors, build bridges and, most importantly, connect talented people with key decision makers

Guardian Angels   Can put up a protective umbrella so that people can act with some freedom, and experiment in relative safety

Wise Owls   The people with organisational know-how and awareness, who help others avoid conflict, understand the politics and navigate around the business

"There is something much more scarce, something rarer than ability. It is the ability to recognise ability."

Robert Half

(36) How do you personally champion talented people?

TALENT
COACH

How can I bring out the best in my people when it matters most?

HARNESSING THE POWER OF TALENT

What mindset do you have when you manage your people?

People often describe talent as needing to be harnessed or channelled.

If you view talent as a river, your role as a talent coach is to channel the water; acting as the banks to guide the water downstream; narrowing the banks at the right time to increase the pace; widening the banks to slow the pace and encourage reflection...but never letting the river stagnate.

> "If managing retention in the past was akin to tending a dam, today it is more like managing a river. The objective is not to stop the water from flowing but to control its direction and speed."
>
> **Peter Cappelli**

TALENT COACH

LESSONS FROM JACK WELCH

Jack Welch was Chief Executive of General Electric for many years, having climbed successfully through the ranks. His beliefs about the role of leadership in developing talent within the business have brought General Electric to the forefront of talent management. Here are some of the lessons all good talent coaches need to learn:

1. **Relax** (and manage less) – stop getting in people's way and looking over their shoulders. Let people perform and you will be surprised at the results.

2. **Instil confidence** – treat people with respect and build confidence in others so they keep things simple.

3. **Think boundary-less** – encourage ideas at all levels and act on them. Get your talent searching for new ideas inside and outside the organisation.

4. **Encourage the stretch** – push for the impossible and encourage people to go beyond ordinary goals. If the goals are not reached, fine, as long as people have truly tried.

5. **Infectious enthusiasm** – for you and all those around you, your customer must always be your passion.

Adapted from *29 Leadership Secrets from Jack Welch*, by Robert Slater

TALENT COACH

WISH FOR WHAT YOU WANT

EXPECTATIONS set BELIEF sets REALITY

It's a simple equation.

What you believe matters. **If you limit your belief in others then you limit their potential**. Nine times out of ten, people limit their own performance because of low self-belief. Your best performers will have a strong self-belief underpinned by technical competence. That 'knowing feeling' in their own abilities means they will consistently exceed expectations. You have a role in developing self-belief in others.

EXPECTATIONS set BELIEF sets REALITY

WISH FOR WHAT YOU WANT

As a talent coach, consciously raising what you expect of others can enhance their performance:

- Encourage your people to set high personal standards
- Always expect the best – stop when you hear yourself doubting others
- Be positive and stay positive – let others know when they start to use negative language
- When performance dips, help people bounce back quickly by expecting a superb performance next time; focus on what went well (especially since talented people are naturally self-critical)
- Ask people what they believe is possible, building on the passion, and help them to describe the practical steps to achieve the dream

THREE TYPES OF GOALS

A manager will help talented people set goals. A great coach will help people set the **right type** of goal and understand the difference. There are three types of goals which alone have little impact but come alive when you bring them together.

Outcome Goals   – dreams, inspiring or ambitious end goals
Performance Goals   – milestones, targets, progress goals
Process Goals   – technique, quality goals

People need dreams to which to aspire. A great coach will help people describe their dreams and stretch what is possible. They will then break these dreams into a series of performance milestones that, if achieved, will make the dreams come true. Progress is rarely in a straight line so the coach will help talent keep focused on the motivating outcome. The coach will also encourage people to focus on the key technical aspects of performance that will deliver a quality performance.

TALENT COACH

SETTING THE BAR

Talented people will naturally aspire to be the best they can be, but everyone needs a little support to set the bar in the ideal place. The following checklist will help you teach others how to set the bar.

1. COMMITMENT

- Get people to list the goals they want to achieve
- Writing down and sharing goals can help create momentum and build commitment
- Encourage them to focus on three to four priorities (the business world often expects complex and multiple goals)

2. UNDERSTANDING

- Ask your people to explain the goals to you
- Listen for the emotions that will explain the underlying motivation – use this knowledge to coach people should energy reduce
- Help differentiate between the types of goals (see previous page)
- Encourage people to be precise and realistic in setting goals

SETTING THE BAR

3. PLANNING

- Start to build the plan together
- Work backwards to break each goal into achievable chunks
- Identify tests, controls and measures that will let you track the milestones that matter most
- If they get off track help them learn and adjust the plan
- Encourage measurement against the best inside and outside the organisation, rather than against people less able

4. SUPPORTING

- Agree your coaching role
- Agree the personal support you will provide
- Identify doors you may need to unlock and hurdles you are well placed to overcome
- Agree when you will revisit the goals and measure progress (make it within six weeks)

PREPARING PEOPLE FOR CHANGE

The negative impact of poorly managed change within organisations can be huge. If change gets a big fanfare, but little else, it's a recipe for failure that can lead to discomfort and resistance. We all know about the change curve and it is your role to help flatten the curve and accelerate the pace through which people achieve acceptance. Then you can start to focus on performance!

> *"Excellence is an art won by training and habituation. We are what we repeatedly do. Excellence, then, is not an act but a habit."*
> **Aristotle**

Denial

Anger/ Frustration

Resistance

Exploration

Acceptance

PREPARING PEOPLE FOR CHANGE

It is important to describe the future destination – the end result of the change. It is also important that you work with people **to plan the journey**, to set realistic targets, provide feedback and help people get back on track when they stray off line.

"The harder I practice and work at my game the luckier I get."
Gary Player, golfer

Yes, it is important that people can learn the behaviours and techniques necessary for future success. It is more important that you create the opportunity for people to practise under pressure and in different environments.

A great coach will prepare talented people for change, instil the importance of practice and coach them through the change.

Skill = Technique under Pressure

A spectator can talk a great game.
A player has the ability to perform.
A talent has the skill to perform under pressure.

THE JOURNEY

One of my favourite analogies for coaching people is the journey. The more challenging the journey, the more skilled you need to be as a coach. Add your own ideas to the themes below:

Destination
You have to be able to describe the destination in a way that inspires others. Paint a picture of a better place – a compelling vision!

Clear Path
How well have you described the route? How easy will it be for others to follow or even guide you? How will you know that you are still on the path? If it gets dark, who will shine the light so you can see the way ahead?

Preparation
How will you get people ready for the journey? What planning, preparation and fitness will increase the likelihood of success? Do they need passports?

THE JOURNEY

Energy
How will you generate the energy and motivation to make others want to follow?
How will you sustain that energy during the journey and who will provide the energy
when you are not around? How quickly will you travel?

Arrival
How will you adjust your path if your destination changes or the path becomes an
impasse? How will you know when you have arrived? What have you learned from the
journey?

Onward Journey
How will you ensure that you have the energy to take on the next challenge, which could
simply be getting down the mountain?

TALENT COACH

STRENGTH BASED DEVELOPMENT

Many development activities are based on traditional *gap analysis* where people are assessed against either an unrealistic expectation, eg perfection, or worse still against average. The resulting development plan seeks to address shortfalls.

A more realistic and positive approach is to accept some weaknesses will be difficult to improve and at best will be managed. This allows you to **focus on developing strengths and improving areas with potential**. In other words, build your greens, strengthen your ambers and manage around your reds.

Development traffic lights

Accept and manage

Develop

Talk about, build and use

STRENGTH BASED DEVELOPMENT

With the development traffic lights in mind you can use the following to have a more constructive development conversation:

- Identify and fully discuss *green* strengths – spend time emphasising the areas they are best at and build self-esteem (so they'll accept tougher feedback later)

- Build on or more fully develop strengths to compensate for weaknesses, eg being an excellent coach means you can get the best from creative people, even if you are not creative yourself

- Provide opportunities for these strengths to be used within your business, eg look for projects that need great change managers

- Identify *amber* opportunities that are important either to role or aspirations and put in place development activities

- Agree *red* weaknesses and plan how best to avoid or manage around these

STIMULATE CREATIVITY

What do you do to stimulate your best people?

If you don't trust your people you naturally limit both performance and creativity – why would they want to take the risks necessary to excel? Many managers will take the safe option when managing others and over-control the detail, leading to short-sighted answers. If you effectively treat your employees as an extra pair of hands they will do little more than you ask.

It's also human nature for people to assume that certain rules exist, eg *I have to sit at my desk; everyone else does and no-one has told me that I can go for a walk*. Creativity is about being different from the crowd, in how you think and how you act.

TALENT COACH

STIMULATING ENVIRONMENT

What can you do to provide a more stimulating environment?

Encourage people to:

- Challenge the barriers to when work takes place, eg time and location
- Question the process
- Have fun!
- Relax and slow down – that's when the sparks fly
- Break habits and get uncomfortable for a while
- Have direct contact with people
- Book time to think into the diary
- Read, travel and walk around

What three things could you do to increase your own energy at work? Ask your talented people the same question.

WHY COACHING WORKS

Coaching focuses on how people can develop and implement their own ideas and practical solutions – translating goals into action. It is about increasing personal responsibility and encouraging people to take ownership of the issues, the very traits that differentiate talented people from others.

There are many coaching models and most have similar stages to those listed here:

Goals into action

STAGE	AIM
Identify issues	Awareness and interest
Set goals	Responsibility
Generate options	Discovery
Agree boundaries	Ownership and consistency
Understand power	Freedom and interdependence
Review success	Learning
Take action	Performance

Find yourself a coaching model you feel comfortable with and use it – every day!

(53)

TALENT COACH

UNDERPERFORMANCE

Even your best people can be stopped in their tracks by complacent management.
When your talent doesn't perform, use this checklist to identify what action, within your
control, will make the difference.

1. Task clarity   Do they know what *good* looks like?

2. Task priority   Do they understand the impact of what they are doing?

3. Competence   Do they have the skills to do the job?

4. Obstacles   What are the real or imagined procedural barriers (rules) that are getting in the way?

5. Reward for failure   Are your decisions rewarding the wrong behaviour?

6. Performance feedback   Are you providing consistent and timely feedback on how they are doing?

7. Role/Person mismatch   Have you put them in the right job or team?

8. OK, they are being wilful!   Let people know the consequences

TALENT COACH

MOVING TOWARDS SUCCESS

At a basic level, people's motivation to perform can be described as either 'towards' or 'away from', ie they are motivated to generate or to avoid a particular emotion. For example, one person may work hard to prepare a presentation because they enjoy the 'buzz' of people valuing their contribution. Another person may prepare equally well for the same presentation to avoid appearing ill-informed.

Listen carefully to your people (a common theme in this book) and you should be able to spot the underlying motivation, the strength of the emotion and whether it is a positive force. As a talent coach you should encourage:

1. A positive 'towards' articulation of the motivation – a healthier place to start.
2. Alignment of team and individual goals with the main motivational drivers.
3. Reflection on achievements; putting into words how success feels helps people to understand themselves better. They can then 'bottle' the emotion for use when they next need a boost.

TALENT COACH

SPITZER'S EIGHT DESIRES OF MOTIVATION

Everyone is motivated differently so it is vital that you know what makes your best people tick. A skilled manager will take every opportunity to hit the motivational 'hot buttons' of their people. Spitzer identified eight different motivators for individuals.

Power
Motivated by status, control of their future and opportunities to progress.

Activity
Motivated by interest and variety in their work.

Recognition
Needs praise and to be acknowledged for good work, and given guidance when they go wrong.

Affiliation
Motivated by social contact, friendship and team spirit.

Competence
Likes to use their strengths, address their weaknesses and learn from mistakes.

Ownership
Needs to get involved and be part of decisions that affect their job.

Meaning
Needs to feel that they have a definite role in the team and a positive contribution to make, gaining a sense of worth from their work.

Achievement
Needs to feel challenged and developed at work, with realistic goals to achieve.

SPITZER'S EIGHT DESIRES OF MOTIVATION

You may know your people well enough to identify their two or three key motivators. If not, or if you wish to help them better understand their own drivers, then try this exercise.

Step 1
Ask them to write on Post-it notes 10 things that really excite and motivate them.

Step 2
Ask them to associate the items on their list with the eight desires.

Step 3
Ask them to identify which ones feature most often and decide on their two or three main motivators.

Step 4
Ask them to identify elements of their current role which satisfy the key motivators and what could be done differently to increase their motivation.

Name	Justine	Julie	Jamal
Power	✔		
Recognition	✔	✔	✔
Competence			✔
Meaning	✔		
Activity		✔	
Affiliation		✔	
Ownership			
Achievement			✔

Please tick which motivators you believe apply to your staff – how can you use this information better to coach them?

TALENT COACH

GROWING A COACHING RELATIONSHIP

Coaching is never a static relationship and, in reality, movement is exactly what you should be aiming towards. Frank Dick talks about the coaching relationship changing over time as the individual grows in self-belief and self-awareness.

Phase	Relationship
Accepting	Coach says, *'this is what you do'*.
Exploring	Individual starts to ask questions to understand. Coach shares thinking.
Challenge	Individual has drive and ambition to make well-expressed and timely challenge. Coach listens and responds positively.
Winner	Individual has strong emotions about performance and result. Coach challenges.
Champion	Individual wishes to leave a legacy.
Legend	Individual wants to be remembered for the quality of winning.

Do you have confidence in your own ability to let the relationship grow?

Do you know when to pass the coaching relationship on to someone better placed?

TALENT COACH

WORK LIFE BALANCE

Talented staff can limit their long-term performance and value to the business, and damage their health by running out of positive energy owing to a lack of work life balance. They can become obsessed with achieving results at work – regardless of anything else! This can have a negative and destructive impact on other areas of their lives.

Talent managers who are excellent at coaching for work life balance:

- Discuss life outside work to give a picture of their lives 'in the round'
- Identify passion and interests outside the workplace
- Adapt work to fit lifestyle issues
- Ensure their talented staff only work late on an exceptional basis
- Set a good example by not working late too often themselves
- Encourage and review achievement of goals inside and outside work

TALENT COACH

WORK LIFE BALANCE

Talent managers are also quick to spot the early triggers of talented staff with poor work life balance:

- Consistently working late
- Accepting more work than they can healthily manage
- Looking increasingly tired or unhealthy
- Losing their patience or becoming unusually irritated

Provided by Richard Lowe

TALENT COACH

MENTORING

Coaching is a powerful management style to adopt with talented people. However, the personal change that the individual may go through as a result means that he or she may also need to find a suitable mentor.

So, what is the difference?

Coaching	Mentoring
Zoom lens/close up	Wide angle lens
Results	Values and vision
Performance	Potential
Short-term	Long-term
Focused on detail	Change in perspective
Specific	Eclectic
Gets you to find answers	Provides advice on shortcuts

TALENT COACH

TESTING HIGH PERFORMERS

How your best people respond when challenged with extra work is a relatively strong indicator of potential.

In his book *'The Peter Principle'*, Dr Laurence J Peter describes the effect when a person with strong technical ability gets promoted, based solely on performance, to a management position and fails. The different mindset required in the management role means that the new job doesn't suit the individual.

Can you plot each of your people using the circles below? The final two describe visually how a high performer may respond to the challenge of additional responsibilities. The final picture is what you would expect with true talent and readiness.

Not yet full performance

Full performance

Inappropriate response

Exceptional performance

TALENT COACH

POSITIVE ROLE MODELS

A great deal of informal learning is as a result of good and bad role models. To help your best people tap into this learning, encourage them to watch others carefully and take the time to reflect on what they see, hear and feel.

Try this exercise. Think about the most memorable and impressive colleague you have known. Name them and identify:

1. What really made them remarkable and memorable?
2. Which of their exceptional strengths had nothing to do with intelligence?
3. What impact did each strength have on you?
4. In what ways did you think or act differently as a result of your contact with them?

If you are not able to find a positive role model you can, of course, complete this exercise based on a bad role model (what not to do!).

TALENT COACH

QUESTIONS FOR TALENTED PEOPLE

An effective approach to managing performance should mean that your people can answer the following questions at any time.

Key questions for review time or when priorities change, eg new role or project

- What are my objectives and how do these contribute to the team objectives?
- What is the stretch for me and the business?
- What support do I need to be successful?
- How can I learn and develop from opportunity?
- How will I know I have been successful and how often will I check I am on track?

Key questions for regular 1-2-1s

- What have I achieved and is this what I promised?
- What didn't get done? What would get me back on track or provide greater stretch?
- How have priorities changed?
- What knowledge or skills do I need to refresh/develop to achieve my objectives?
- Overall, how well am I meeting expectations?

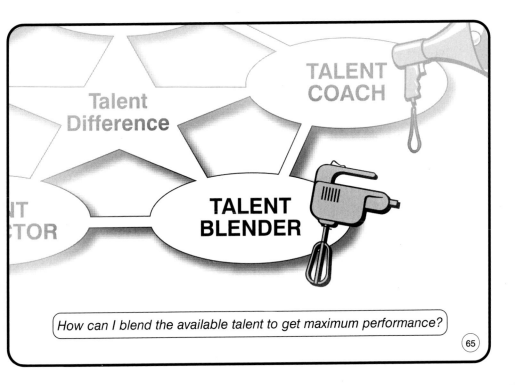

TALENT
COACH

Talent
Difference

NT
CTOR

**TALENT
BLENDER**

How can I blend the available talent to get maximum performance?

TALENT BLENDER

INGREDIENTS FOR A TALENTED TEAM

1. First check the ingredients you already have in the cupboard.
2. Then add quality to the pot, using the best affordable ingredients.
3. Stir the pot and watch carefully as the team raise their game and success attracts others.

TALENT BLENDER

INGREDIENTS FOR A TALENTED TEAM
FIVE TIPS

Check that you have the following:

1. The necessary technical experts in your team – you must be able to deliver your core product and service.

2. A common purpose and understanding within the team of the challenge ahead – talented people are passionate about challenge. This is best looked at as a team so that everyone understands their own contribution, what others will contribute, and they can see a visible shared commitment.

3. Complementary rather than similar personality attributes. While diversity may seem like a more difficult option, the difference and conflict it can create are far more likely to lead to breakthrough performance for your team – it just needs a talented manager.

4. A genuine desire amongst your talented people to help others achieve. They need to work hard and care about the team's results, not just their own.

5. People you feel you can trust – this could be people you have worked with before.

CO-OPERATIVE OR CONTRIBUTORY TEAMS

There are different types of teams. Imagine two ends of a spectrum defined at the extremes as co-operative and contributory. What type of team do you lead? Are you focusing on the best things to drive the performance of your team?

TEAM TYPE	CO-OPERATIVE	CONTRIBUTORY
Examples	Basketball, jazz band, football, customer service, cabin crew.	Cricket, sales teams, remote working, contact centre.
Performance Drivers	Ability to read the game, change positions, think and move for each other and spot the gaps in performance as they happen.	Focus on a common goal, desire to be the best you can, compete constructively with team colleagues, cheer others' success, deliver what you promise and recognise that every contribution matters.

TALENT BLENDER

CO-OPERATIVE OR CONTRIBUTORY TEAMS

Team Values	Your value to the team matters. One person can't win.	Personal targets based on talent and role. One person can make a big difference.
Coach Focus	Get people to play out of position so they understand different perspectives.	Get people to understand the value of own contribution towards a common goal.
	Encourage them to ask for help and look out for each other.	Encourage sharing of techniques and successes.
	Practise team communication and awareness.	Focus on planning ahead and accountability.

CO-OPERATIVE OR CONTRIBUTORY TEAMS

Talented People Must...	Learn to play with each other, regardless of talent.	Recognise everyone matters. Compete constructively and help others learn.
Analogy	A beach ball – every side could be different depending on your perspective.	Cathedral – every brick matters.

TALENT BLENDER

EQUAL TREATMENT FOR UNEQUAL TALENTS

The first lesson for any team leader is to realise that every team member should be treated as an individual and encouraged to make a personal contribution, to the best of their ability.

It is important, however, that you don't take this as a licence to focus solely on your favourite or best people. As a credible leader you must provide equal opportunity (which people may choose to take or not), and encourage others to be responsible for being the best that they can be. Some examples of things that should be provided equally:

✔ Time with you
✔ Access to suitable development opportunities
✔ Opportunity to have their say
✔ Reward for what they contribute

Examples of things that should not be equal:

✗ Actual level of responsibility they have (depends on competence)
✗ Accountability for results (depends on role and reward)
✗ Type of development activity (depends on individual needs)

TALENT BLENDER

INTERDEPENDENCE

Small children are, initially, incredibly dependent. As they grow up they have periods of independence when they push away those they have previously relied on. Later that independence may be replaced with a more **interdependent** approach, when children accept and realise the power of working with others. The same can happen in a team, especially with talented people who are more capable of being independent of others.

Dependent	Independent	Interdependent
You take care of me	I can do it	We can do it
You come through for me	I am responsible	We can co-operate
You didn't come through	I am self-reliant	We can combine our talents and abilities
I blame you for the results	I can choose	We can create something great together
I need others to get what I want	I can get what I want through my own efforts	My own efforts are best combined with the efforts of others to achieve success

As managers we spend time encouraging people to make choices, be accountable, and take responsibility. The danger is that people will hear 'be independent' rather than 'work together'. Think about ways in which you can create interdependence.

TALENT BLENDER

MANAGING PRIMA DONNAS

Talent is:

- A genius for making things happen…
- With a minimum fuss…
- Inspiring others to do the same

What do you do when you have a person with raw talent? A hotheaded, explosive character whose excellence demands a place in the team? A prima donna who will demand your time and could destroy the overall team? Every team can thrive on an injection of talent if the core is well balanced. We know that well respected, strong team members will usually have a positive influence on prima donnas, so you are not on your own. We also know that visible and agreed team values may make self-governance and discipline easier.

However, it's a straight cost benefit analysis, so get out a blank sheet of paper, draw a line down the middle and start listing the pro's and con's. See next page for examples.

TALENT BLENDER

MANAGING PRIMA DONNAS

FOR	AGAINST
✔ Will make a significant difference to our result	✘ Emotional outbursts will upset other team members
✔ Will raise the standard for others	✘ I will need to dedicate more of my time to managing the person and the fallout
✔ Will add drive and energy that has been lacking recently	✘ We may lose other team members
✔ We have someone who could mentor the person	✘ The team aren't cohesive enough to handle someone like this

Your analysis may help you realise that sometimes prima donnas can just be too much of a risk, in which case manage without them, however talented they are!

For more ideas on how best to blend your talented people read the *Teambuilding Activities Pocketbook*.

TALENT BLENDER

A LONG-TERM APPROACH

"I did not set out to build a team: the task ahead was much bigger than that. What I really embarked on was the building of a system which would produce not one team but four or five, each occupying a rung on the ladder, the summit of which was the first XI."

Consider the approach of Sir Matt Busby, the all-time great football manager, to developing his team.

- How do you view developing a team – a marathon or a sprint?

- How well are you using rising talent to provide healthy competition?

- When someone gets a promotion or leaves, what do you have in place to sustain the future success of the team?

TALENT BLENDER

A LONG-TERM APPROACH

Here are some ideas that any manager can adopt to shift to a longer-term, more sustainable approach to developing teams:

- Share the development projects and challenges around
- Rotate jobs even if that means a temporary drop in team performance
- Write things down – excellence is as much to do with great processes as it is the ability of a few great people
- Treat your core well, not just your talented people
- Initiate talent-spotting outside your team – think of it as an internal search. Talk to other managers and look for opportunities to move people around
- Spend some time on teambuilding and cohesion, including the teams and suppliers you work most closely with
- Pace yourself and make time for playing together
- If possible, be flexible about when and where your people work together

TALENT
MAGNET

Talent
Difference

TALENT
CONDUCTOR

T
BL

How can I create a flow of talented people?

TALENT CONDUCTOR

HEALTHY BELIEFS ABOUT TALENT

It is important to know how your senior managers collectively view talent management. Here are some unhealthy beliefs:

- ✗ *Life is about hard knocks so we should make it tough for our people*
- ✗ *Our HR department does a great job managing talent*
- ✗ *The ability to deliver is the only good indicator of potential, other than qualifications, obviously!*

Here are a few healthier ones:

- ✔ Every senior manager is accountable for spotting and developing talented people
- ✔ Developing a talent flow should be part of the business planning timetable
- ✔ Developing future senior managers needs real collaboration between all areas
- ✔ Talented people thrive in a performance culture
- ✔ Talented people learn by being stretched so use them to best effect
- ✔ Overall performance is a blend of the 'what' and 'how'; a shortfall in either must be dealt with quickly

Get views from your senior team and record them; then discuss the impact on the business.

DEFINING PERFORMANCE

Encourage your organisation to take a broad view of performance to include both what gets done (objectives) and how it gets done (behaviours). Once you have undertaken this you can discuss where your organisation draws the lines to define 'best', 'valued' and 'less effective'.

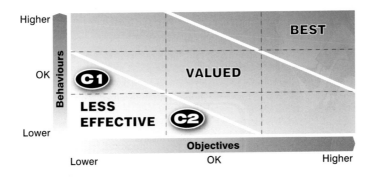

DEFINING PERFORMANCE

Best performers
The very best contributors within the company. Consistently exceed and outpace changing expectations and are role models for our behaviours.

Valued performers
Strong contributors to business performance. Demonstrate our behaviours and keep pace with expectations.

Less effective performers
Least effective contributors. There is a recognised need for improvement in achieving objectives and/or demonstrating behaviours that show values are shared.

If you take the success of your organisation seriously you will act positively to deal with the less effective performers. In many ways the decision is easier with someone who doesn't achieve objectives or demonstrate the expected behaviours – they have to shape up very quickly or leave. The borderline decisions are tougher. Some advice:

 Give them another chance in another role

 Tough call, but you probably need to replace them

TALENT CONDUCTOR

TALENT PROFILER

It is important that the decisions you take about your
talented people are well informed, eg investing in
training, the nature and timing of their next move. What
information do you need at your fingertips? What is the
talent profile you need for each person in your team?

> "Simplicity is the ultimate
> sophistication."
> **Leonardo da Vinci**

The following four areas are a good place to start building a talent profile.

Track Record   What they **can** do
Potential Predictors What they **could** do
Personal Aspirations What they **want** to do
Readiness   When they will be **ready** to do it

Once you have a talent profile you can start to grapple with other questions such as:

- Who else needs to see the profile
- How you can keep the information current and accurate
- Who should own the profile
- How transparent the information should be

TALENT PROFILER

TRACK RECORD		**POTENTIAL PREDICTORS**		**PERSONAL ASPIRATIONS**		**READINESS**
What do we already know about someone that is relevant to profiling potential?	**+**	Predictors of whether someone has the potential to succeed in a bigger and/or more senior role	**+**	An indication of an individual's personal ambition and interest	**=**	An indication of the readiness of someone to make the next move and to what level

The following pages will show how to build your own talent profile

TALENT CONDUCTOR

TRACK RECORD

There are three distinct areas that come together to create a track record of performance.

Achievement **What have they done?**
Attitude **How did they bring it about?**
Ability **What knowledge and skills did they display?**

The achievement of agreed objectives, the personal contribution someone makes, eg projects completed, usually provides a good assessment of **achievement**, often stated as a performance rating.

In a similar way, **attitude** is often assessed against a predetermined set of expected and observable competencies or behaviours.

Ability is the proven and relevant knowledge and skills developed from experience, eg effectively managing remote teams.

Every organisation will have its own ways of tracking achievement, attitude and ability. What information should you have at your fingertips about track record?

TALENT CONDUCTOR

INDICATORS OF POTENTIAL

A strong track record alone is not a great predictor of future success at a higher level. Often good people are promoted just one step too far and are set up for failure and frustration. It is possible with research, however, to identify which traits are reasonably good predictors of success within your organisation. The examples below are based on research within one organisation – what are your predictors?

	Track Record	Indicators of Potential
Achievement	Achievement of performance objectives	✔ Handles pressure effectively and makes the job look easy ✔ Challenges the boundaries of role. Keen to take on new, bigger challenges ✔ Orientated towards business results, not just focused on success of own area
Attitude	Demonstration of desirable behaviours	✔ Confidence to take the lead ✔ Determined, resilient and prepared to be unpopular ✔ Natural enthusiasm and positive outlook ✔ Credible interpersonal skills with people at all levels in the company
Ability	Evidence of knowledge and skills	✔ Understands and acts quickly and effectively in new/complex situations ✔ Receptive and open to new ideas and feedback and adapts how they work ✔ Exhibits technical and professional skills that are both broad and deep

TALENT CONDUCTOR

READINESS

Everyone contributes to success and is capable of more but only some have the potential to perform in a larger role. Honest, accurate assessment and feedback are at the heart of managing talent. In determining readiness you need to bring together an assessment of potential and the time required to achieve it. How do you want to describe and categorise potential? What language exists or would work in your organisation? The following example takes the position that everyone has at least some potential:

- **High potential** – very likely to compete successfully for, and succeed in, higher level roles within two years
- **Growth potential** – expect to be able to succeed in larger jobs at a similar level, with potential to move upwards in the longer term
- **Stretch potential** – likely to remain in position or move to a role with similar responsibilities; will develop expertise.

Don't forget about personal aspirations: it is essential for any talent manager to know what drives an individual. There is no science to this – simply ask them. The accuracy of the self-assessment is improved by the quality of feedback they have had and the openness of your relationship. **Without aspiration, potential is of little value**.

NINE BOX MODEL – AIRLINE STYLE

The nine box model is a talent management classic, first used in General Electric. Simply by combining an assessment of potential and performance you can better differentiate your talent strategies.

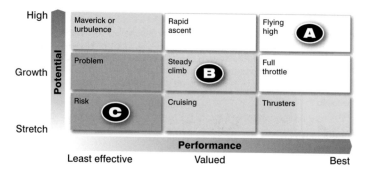

	Least effective	Valued	Best
High	Maverick or turbulence	Rapid ascent	Flying high **A**
Growth	Problem	Steady climb **B**	Full throttle
Stretch	Risk **C**	Cruising	Thrusters

Potential (vertical axis)

Performance (horizontal axis)

TALENT CONDUCTOR

THE A, B, C's

The power of the nine box model comes when you are able to consistently apply the approach across the whole organisation – everyone understands the definitions and implications of the placement within the nine boxes. At its best senior managers will complete the exercise as part of the strategic timetable – determining the bench strength of the organisation, level by level.

The placement of people within the model should be subject to challenge and agreement from the wider leadership team. In many ways the discussion about talent and the transparency it creates is more powerful than the placement itself.

The nine box model must lead to decisions about talent.
For example:

 Retain at all costs, leaders to watch and stretch

 Keep if you can and develop

 Improve or lose

TALENT CONDUCTOR

PLACE YOUR BETS

What kind of talent do you have on your hands? Sometimes you don't have the luxury of promoting the perfect candidate. Where would you place your bet if the picture was less than perfect?

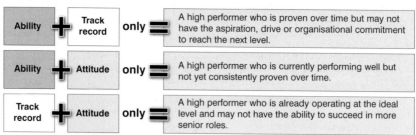

Ability + Track record	only =	A high performer who is proven over time but may not have the aspiration, drive or organisational commitment to reach the next level.
Ability + Attitude	only =	A high performer who is currently performing well but not yet consistently proven over time.
Track record + Attitude	only =	A high performer who is already operating at the ideal level and may not have the ability to succeed in more senior roles.

Ability and attitude would be a strong bet – with the individual having the opportunity to develop a track record. How often do we pick the track record as the best indicator of potential?

TALENT CONDUCTOR

ASSESSMENT

Many talent management activities involve the need to confidently assess people's potential or performance. There are many ways to do this, and an equally diverse range of tools and techniques, ranging from manager assessment to psychologist designed assessment centres. How to assess is beyond the scope of this book, but here are some top tips to make assessment more readily accepted by those being assessed.

- Be clear how the assessment will be used, eg to decide development priorities vs selection for promotion
- Keep the assessment real – ground it in the context and pressures of the business
- Always provide quality feedback
- Build a robust personal development plan for all involved, not just those successful

- Celebrate the strengths identified
- Involve non-HR people in the assessment and invest in assessor training
- Keep it balanced – use 'track record' information as well as what you learn from the assessment process
- Consider the message you send to those who are not successful and who aren't selected for assessment – they'll know who they are

TALENT CONDUCTOR

PEBBLES – POLISH OR PICK

When you look at a beach you see pebbles – piles of dull stones all looking much the same. You know that amongst them will be pebbles with amazing colours and fantastic shapes – you just need to polish them! Where do you start? Do you pick a few pebbles that look promising and give them a polish, accepting that you won't always make the right choice, or polish as many as you can straight away.

Your decision whether to 'pick and polish' or 'polish and pick' is an early one you need to make in any talent management approach. Do you invest your money in assessment of a select few or do you invest in broader development allowing the best to shine through?

If you are interested in the following, then pick before you polish:

✔ Confirming potential
✔ Targeting development investment
✔ Guiding placement and selection decisions

If you are interested in the following, then polish before you pick:

✔ Building capability in the organisation
✔ Getting people ready for a job challenge
✔ Developing competencies
✔ Identifying personality traits

TALENT CONDUCTOR

LETTING YOUR TALENT KNOW

Do you let your talented people know they are earmarked as high potential? Do they already know? Who else needs to know and will others find out? How transparent do you make your decisions? Letting people know has the following advantages and disadvantages:

Advantages
✔ Motivating for talent
✔ Public recognition for people
✔ Focuses the minds of nominating managers
✔ Something to work towards
✔ Gives out message that company values talent – aids recruitment

Disadvantages
✘ Demotivating for others; those not picked out feel undervalued
✘ Weak managers may avoid tough decisions
✘ Creates higher expectations in those selected
✘ Your talent may develop prima donna tendencies
✘ Will expose frailties in basis of selection, eg performance

The decision will be influenced by what is on offer as a result of selection, eg: accelerated development, reward, number of people involved in the assessment, openness of company culture and expectation of employees.

TALENT CONDUCTOR

SUPPORT KEY TRANSITIONS

Promotions rarely lead to a smooth progression. The step change between some roles can make it difficult to adapt quickly. This is particularly the case if the change is of one of the key transitions, eg from managing self to managing people or from managing people to managing managers.

As mentioned on page 62, **performance in one role is not always a good predictor of performance in another**. It is these transitions that demand a fundamental change in what you value, your skills and perspective.

When developing talented people you must be aware of the challenges facing the individual. Looking at the example of someone making the transition from managing self to managing others you can ask:

1. Which values will drive success in the new role?
   Eg: *Making time for others*

2. What are the key new skills in the role?
   Eg: *Providing constructive feedback*

3. What perspective will be most valuable in the future?
   Eg: *Beyond the next 12 months*

Adapted from: The Leadership Pipeline

TALENT CONDUCTOR

SUCCESSION MANAGEMENT

Many companies like to put in place a succession plan – an elegant map of the organisation showing named successors and *just in case* people, with every risk identified and contingency plans in place. Is this a valuable use of time or a source of false confidence based on what appears to be a complete picture?

Organisations need to be able to respond rapidly to change and can no longer rely on the most talented people waiting patiently for the next step. Even the best laid plans can unravel over a relatively short period of time as roles and people change.

An alternative is to take a risk management approach to succession:

- Agree the roles which are key to future business success
- Determine the *what if* scenarios for each key role
- List the roles appearing to lack strength in depth and put in place a *talent flow* towards them
- Provide broad development opportunities based on an individual's aspirations
- Select the best available person when a vacancy does arise

TALENT CONDUCTOR

TALENT FORUM

Senior managers clearly have the accountability for talent management in any organisation. What forum do you have in place for the necessary conversations to take place and how often should the forum be convened? Consider the potential agenda items below and decide on the focus of your talent forum:

- Review the impact of your business strategy and key projects on the talent you need
- Review company culture eg employee opinion survey
- Challenge and benchmark the profile of performance ratings
- Assess the bench strength for senior and key roles
- Create space for development eg secondments, projects, rotation
- Make reward, bonus and recognition programme decisions
- Review key measures eg diversity, internal promotions and moves
- Agree the focus for 'development agenda' and resources for next period
- Develop a 'talent to watch' list and agree who will stay close to these people
- Hold the next level down accountable for shifting the 'C' list performers quickly

TALENT CONDUCTOR

EMBEDDING TALENT MANAGEMENT INTO BUSINESS PLANNING

Just how important is talent management in your organisation? A good test is the extent to which the practices associated with it have been embedded into the business planning process. Follow the steps below for a good way to do this.

1. **List all the business activities that exist in your organisation, eg:**
   Strategy – development, communication and review
   Operational – planning, cascading, budgeting and forecasting
   Communications – executive level, operating reviews and conferences
   Performance – setting and reviewing performance objectives, 360 feedback and development planning
   People – employee survey and action planning, reward and recognition activities

2. **Draw a 12 month timeline and transfer each business activity to the appropriate part of the timeline**

EMBEDDING TALENT MANAGEMENT INTO BUSINESS PLANNING

3. **Identify the dependencies between each activity**
   eg strategy development before operational planning

4. **Identify bottlenecks and opportunities to better align talent activities**
   eg employee survey results before operational planning, 360 feedback before strategic talent review

Share your map with others and agree on the best possible fit.

TALENT CONDUCTOR

FIVE DEVELOPMENT EXPERIENCES

According to Helen Handfield-Jones, *How Executives Grow*, the following five experiences provide the stretch to accelerate the development of leadership talent.

1. A new job with greater scope
2. Turning a business around
3. Starting a business
4. Managing a large project
5. Working abroad

All talented people thrive on experiences which provide:

- Early leadership roles and significant responsibilities
- Increased pressure under which to try out skills
- Visual accountability for fix-it situations and results
- An opportunity to build and lead a team in tough situations
- Strong coaching and speedy feedback
- Cross functional and cross cultural experiences so you can learn from differences
- Encouragement to take risks with a soft(er) landing to help learning

> *"I hear and I forget, I see and I remember, I do and I understand"*
> Confucius

TALENT CONDUCTOR

TALENT SCORECARD

How do you measure the success of your talent management activities?

- % of your people who, if they applied today, would be picked
- Number of long-term vacancies
- Average time taken to fill vacancies
- Employee retention rates for key roles, performance levels and departments
- Balance between internal and external appointments
- Spend on contingent workers and consultants
- Quality perception of hiring managers
- Stakeholder satisfaction
- Quality of recruits, eg average time taken to reach competence
- Employee engagement index
- Shift in 360 degree or other feedback scores
- % people classified as A, B and C list
- % key roles with more than one potential internal replacement
- % people with a personal development plan
- Diversity and inclusion rates

TALENT MAGNET

ATTRACT OR REPEL?

The big question is, *'why would talented people want to join your organisation?'*

How your organisation is seen in the outside world – your reputation – is something that will either act as a positive force to attract great employees or will repel the best from joining you. Answer these questions to develop an image of your reputation.

1. At your worst, how would your organisation or team be described?
2. When you shine, how would your organisation or team be described?
3. What does your organisation or team represent?
4. What makes your organisation or team stand out from your competitors?
5. What is the public image of your leadership team?

What conclusions can you draw from your answers? Are you describing an attractive employer, a company or team people would want to be associated with? What score out of 10 would you realistically give yourself? (0 = stinker, 10 = attractive). The lower your score the more likely you are to have to buy or grow your own talent. To reduce this likelihood (and expense) you may decide you need to actively manage your reputation.

STICKY RECRUITMENT: TOP TIPS

The recruitment process is important, not just in making the best selection but also in bonding talent to the company. Recruiting should be *sticky* and the following will help you keep your best people even before you start.

- Involve your team in the process – talented people want to know who will help them realise their potential
- Provide an honest preview of the job – the talented thrive on a challenge or a fix-it situation
- Set the bar high – profile the company's successes and strengths so that talented people can see what they will learn; don't be modest!
- Explore and share values and motives – your company's, your own and the individual's. Overlap = stickiness
- Know your company's talent predictors – what your best people have got in common – and look for evidence in the interview
- Treat people well at recruitment – candidates are looking for clues about you and your organisation. Actively manage expectations and show as realistic a picture as possible. Talented people like to see a challenge

GOOD RECRUITMENT PRACTICES

Man of the Match or Mates of Mine? Who gets the promotion and how the decision is made can make or break confidence in how your organisation manages talent. While a hiring manager must feel comfortable with whoever they appoint and may have invested in the development of some candidates, the final decision should always be the best affordable person. The following recruitment principles will encourage the best use of your talented people:

- Explore alternatives to permanent replacement to broaden their accountabilities
- Search the talent pool – based on specific aspirations and track record to identify 'hidden' talent outside your own team – to consider alongside talent within your area
- Advertise all new and replacement roles internally and externally
- Talk to your talent champions (see page 36)
- Consider evidence of personal development a positive indicator for selection and be prepared to take a *nearly ready* internal candidate and help them develop
- Ensure rigorous assessment of track record and potential at recruitment stage; no shortcuts

TALENT MAGNET

LOVE TO WORK

We would all prefer a happy workplace but in itself it is not enough.
Those happy people may not be the ones who really respond
under pressure, willingly share ideas and challenge how you
operate; the people you can trust in tough times. Get beyond
happy and into **engaged**, spread a little love – that's what
drives performance.

1. What do your best people **think** about your organisation?
2. How do your best people **feel** about your organisation?
3. What are your best people **willing to do** for your organisation?

In the diagram, the Cognitive or Think component relates to employees'
logical evaluation of a company's goals and values. The Affective or Feel
component taps into whether employees have a sense of belonging and pride.
Finally, the Behavioural or Act dimension captures the outcomes that employers
desire, eg retention and willingness to go the extra distance when necessary.
Engagement itself is actually a measure of the combination of these three components.

TALENT MAGNET

LOVE TO WORK

Some good questions to ask yourself or your people.

Think
- Do I believe in the vision and strategic ambitions of our organisation?
- Do I share the values for which our organisation stands?

Feel
- Am I proud to be part of this organisation?
- Would I recommend this organisation as a good employer?

Act
- Would it take much for me to look for another job elsewhere?
- Am I willing to put in extra effort for the organisation when it really matters?

You can ask these questions individually in focus groups, or ideally as part of a more complete employee opinion survey.

Thanks to ISR. To find out more visit www.isrinsight.com

WHAT MAKES TALENTED PEOPLE (S)TICK?

Talented people are naturally engaged and committed to success. When that loyalty fades and your best people leave or switch teams it doesn't mean their talent has faded. Managers with low magnetism will blame higher salaries or the predictable need for career progression.

The real reasons are more likely to be:
- Not getting the challenge that they crave
- Not being supported to achieve personal ambitions
- Not sharing the values of the company or the manager
- Not being cared for as an individual

Identify your best people and ask yourself:
- What challenges does this person have now?
- What challenges can I provide in the future?
- How can I explain the challenges in a compelling way?
- How can I prepare this person for the challenge and support them to achieve it?

Talented people expect recognition and reward for what they do. It is a good idea to differentiate the reward and recognition that someone can receive when they deliver results. In particular, try to balance the attention you pay to results and to the methods used to achieve them.

TALENT MAGNET

EXCITING JOBS

**Talk to your best people to find out what makes them buzz.
How does your list compare?**

- The opportunity to 'move' when the personal challenge reduces
- Plenty of freedom, autonomy and responsibility
- Open doors that lead to talented and competent (role model) leaders
- Stimulating colleagues
- The space to try things, build on ideas and find solutions
- Someone who will show an interest in them and how they are doing
- A personal stretch but not defeat
- A steady flow of new ideas and projects
- Being able to make a direct and significant contribution to the business
- A fair wage **and** the tools to do the job

Your job as a talent manager is to listen carefully and spot the opportunities to create more buzz. What would make *your* workplace even more stimulating and motivating?

TALENT MAGNET

HOW ATTRACTIVE IS YOUR TALENT CULTURE?

The following are questions talented people regularly ask themselves. How would your best people answer the questions?

	YES	NO
1. Can I learn from my manager?	◯	◯
2. Do I know what is next for me?	◯	◯
3. Can this organisation provide a fresh challenge and stretch?	◯	◯
4. Can this organisation provide progression?	◯	◯
5. Is there a problem that needs solving?	◯	◯
6. Is this undertaking worthwhile?	◯	◯
7. Do I feel comfortable with the values of this organisation?	◯	◯
8. Do I get recognition for my efforts?	◯	◯
9. Am I adding value here?	◯	◯
10. Do I respect and value the people I am working with?	◯	◯
11. Do I have the freedom to get on with my job?	◯	◯
12. Can I be flexible in how, when and where I work?	◯	◯

TALENT MAGNET

HOW ATTRACTIVE IS YOUR TALENT CULTURE?

	YES	NO
13. Do I have the freedom to experiment, make mistakes and learn?	◯	◯
14. Do I receive regular, honest, and candid feedback?	◯	◯
15. Do I feel good about myself and what I am doing?	◯	◯
16. Am I enjoying this?	◯	◯
17. Am I stimulated?	◯	◯

How would your best people score your team?

0 to 5   They have probably dusted off the CV and you'll need to act quickly and honestly to persuade them to stick around.

6 to 12   Good job! You are likely to be attractive to talented people but complacency may be your undoing. Check out the areas you didn't score as Yes and find a way to shift your score upwards.

13 to 17   Such is your attractiveness you must be turning great people away. Congratulations, please share your expertise with others in your organisation.

TALENT MAGNET

FINAL THOUGHTS

So what is the future for talent? There is much that will influence how we get the best from our talented people. For example, technology and legislation will drive an agenda of flexible working practices. Global and environmental challenges will influence the perspective of people away from traditional ways of working.

My final thoughts have to be about being flexible and responsive when defining how you will work with your talented people. Be flexible about how you expect them to work, when and where you want them to work and even the work you ask them to do.

Remember:
- Variety is naturally refreshing and change itself broadens perspective as you learn from differences
- Flexibility encourages people to explore more and see things afresh
- Relaxation is one of the best ways to stimulate creativity (just think about how your mind wanders in the shower or when you're exercising)

I hope this book has stimulated some ideas and inspired you to do things differently.

Good luck!

BOOKS WORTH READING

There are many great talent managers out there and almost as many books. Here are some I have enjoyed:

Winning: Motivation for Business, Sport & Life, Frank Dick, OBE, Abingdon Pub, 1992

Coaching for Performance, Sir John Whitmore, Nicholas Brealey, 2002

Grow your own Leaders, William C Byham, Audrey B Smith & Matthew J Paese, Financial Times Prentice Hall, 2002

The Leadership Pipeline, Ram Charan, Stephen J Drotter & James L Noel, Jossey-Bass, 2001

29 Leadership Secrets from Jack Welch, Robert Slater, McGraw-Hill, 2003

The War for Talent, Ed Michaels, Helen Handfield-Jones & Beth Axelrod, Harvard Business School Press, 2001

The War for Talent: Getting the best from the best, Michael R Williams, Institute of Personnel and Development, 2000

Teambuilding Activities Pocketbook, Paul Tizzard, Management Pocketbooks, 2006

Mind Games: Inspirational Lessons from the World's Finest Sports Stars, Jeff Grout & Sarah Perrin, Capstone, 2006

About the Author

Andy Cross

Andy is Head of Organisation and People Development at Virgin Atlantic. With a diverse background in financial services, customer services and consultancy, Andy loves sharing ideas with others and helping people, teams and organisations to perform.

Andy's passion for growing talent extends to his love of his family and sport – trying to keep up with the kids and to slow down the transition from player of many sports to coach of a few.

Contact

Andy can be contacted at Virgin Atlantic or email andycross@ntlworld.com
83 Somerset Road
Meadvale
Reigate
RH1 6ND
01737 224326

ORDER FORM

Your details

Name _____

Position _____

Company _____

Address _____

_____

_____

Telephone _____

Fax _____

E-mail _____

VAT No. (EC companies) _____

Your Order Ref _____

Please send me:

		No. copies
The Talent Management	Pocketbook	☐
The _____	Pocketbook	☐
The _____	Pocketbook	☐
The _____	Pocketbook	☐
The _____	Pocketbook	☐

Order by Post

MANAGEMENT POCKETBOOKS LTD

LAUREL HOUSE, STATION APPROACH,
ALRESFORD, HAMPSHIRE SO24 9JH UK

Order by Phone, Fax or Internet

Telephone: +44 (0)1962 735573
Facsimile: +44 (0)1962 733637
E-mail: sales@pocketbook.co.uk
Web: www.pocketbook.co.uk

MANAGEMENT POCKETBOOKS